Documenting Intelligence Mission- Data Production Requirements

How the U.S. Department of Defense Can Improve Efficiency and Effectiveness by Streamlining the Production Requirement Process

BRADLEY KNOPP, DAVID LUCKEY, YULIYA SHOKH

Prepared for the Air Intelligence Requirements Task Force
Approved for public release; distribution unlimited

NATIONAL DEFENSE RESEARCH INSTITUTE

For more information on this publication, visit www.rand.org/t/RRA241-1

Library of Congress Cataloging-in-Publication Data is available for this publication.
ISBN: 978-1-9774-0624-8

Published by the RAND Corporation, Santa Monica, Calif.
© Copyright 2021 RAND Corporation
RAND® is a registered trademark.

Cover images by monsitj/Adobe Stock;
Mass Communication Specialist 2nd Class Charlotte C. Oliver/U.S. Navy

Limited Print and Electronic Distribution Rights

This document and trademark(s) contained herein are protected by law. This representation of RAND intellectual property is provided for noncommercial use only. Unauthorized posting of this publication online is prohibited. Permission is given to duplicate this document for personal use only, as long as it is unaltered and complete. Permission is required from RAND to reproduce, or reuse in another form, any of its research documents for commercial use. For information on reprint and linking permissions, please visit www.rand.org/pubs/permissions.

The RAND Corporation is a research organization that develops solutions to public policy challenges to help make communities throughout the world safer and more secure, healthier and more prosperous. RAND is nonprofit, nonpartisan, and committed to the public interest.

RAND's publications do not necessarily reflect the opinions of its research clients and sponsors.

Support RAND
Make a tax-deductible charitable contribution at
www.rand.org/giving/contribute

www.rand.org

Preface

The authors of this report examine issues relating to the identification of requirements for Intelligence Mission Data (IMD) and intelligence production. They examined several questions posed by the sponsor, the director of the Air Intelligence Requirements Task Force:

1. Are there policy changes that would reduce inefficiency in the processes?
2. What are the equities of the stakeholders (i.e., customers and producers)?
3. What is the optimal way to draft input to the Community On-Line System for End Users and Managers database? When is a production requirement necessary?
4. Can improvements in the assembly and communication of IMD requirements increase timeliness and quality of IMD production?

This research should be of interest to the military services and combatant commanders who request IMD to support acquisition and operational planning and to the elements of the intelligence community responsible for collecting and producing IMD. The research reported here was completed in July 2018 and underwent security review with the Defense Office of Prepublication and Security Review before public release.

This research was sponsored by the director of Air Intelligence Requirements Task Force and that organization's sponsors in the the Joint Staff, and the intelligence community and conducted within the Cyber and Intelligence Policy Center of the RAND National Security Research Division (NSRD), which operates the National Defense Research Institute (NDRI), a federally funded research and development center sponsored by the Office of the Secretary of Defense, the Joint Staff, the Unified Combatant Commands, the Navy, the Marine Corps, the defense agencies, and the defense intelligence enterprise.

For more information on the RAND Cyber and Intelligence Policy Center, see www.rand.org/nsrd/intel or contact the director (contact information is provided on the webpage).

Contents

Figures

Tables

Summary

The Acquisition Intelligence Requirements Task Force (AIRTF) asked RAND Corporation researchers to examine the process for developing, validating, and tasking Intelligence Mission Data (IMD) requirements.[1] In response, we prepared process maps depicting the current methods used to identify and manage IMD requirements and researched a set of process-improvement questions that arose from a continuous process improvement (CPI) meeting attended by IMD stakeholders.

AIRTF was established in part to manage the identification of IMD requirements and to improve the quality and timeliness of the intelligence community's response to IMD intelligence production requirements. Previous AIRTF efforts focused on gaining a complete understanding of the process for identifying IMD requirements for military equipment that was being acquired or currently fielded. There are several processes associated with this work, and stakeholders understand that the processes are inefficient or unworkable. In August 2018, AIRTF hosted a CPI seminar with stakeholders to try to identify significant "pain points"—specific problems—in the process. Numerous impediments were identified on both the requirement-identification and intelligence production sides of the issue.

AIRTF requested that we review a production requirement (PR) for IMD production through the "bureaucracy"—from initiation to response—to determine if efficiencies and effectiveness in the process could be maximized. To address this question effectively, we chose

---

[1] An extended discussion of IMD and the definition of the term is found in Chapter One.

to review the handling of PRs resulting from a Life-Cycle Mission Data Plan (LMDP) against ad hoc requirements, because LMDP requirements data are more easily accessed and reliable than data on ad hoc requirements. Our analysis sought to validate the hypothesis that efficiencies could be gained by minimizing processing effort and backlog by combining requests.

AIRTF also asked that we review the use of the Community On-Line System for End Users and Managers (COLISEUM)[2] as the tasking vehicle for production. We pursued a theme of determining if efficiencies could be realized by gaining a better understanding of the business rules of COLISEUM and of the Defense Intelligence Analysis Program, which determines who produces what in the intelligence community.

AIRTF leaders also sought more data on how LMDPs are processed through the IMD Management, Analysis, and Reporting System (IMARS) and another task-management system, the Acquisition Intelligence Requirements Visualization Enterprise Workflows (AIRViEW). This review aimed to try to understand and correct persistent issues or at least provide workarounds to those impediments. We also sought to confirm that intelligence personnel are managing and validating the IMARS system, its processes, and the input. More specifically, we aimed to determine if there should be requirement managers for the process, and, if so, who should be trained and how should they be trained? In addition to these basic questions, we addressed five specific research questions and, in the process of answering these questions, we made several observations and suggestions.

Research Questions

1. Are there policy changes that would reduce inefficiency in the processes?

---

[2] COLISEUM is the system used to task Intelligence Production Centers for finished intelligence.

2. What are the equities of the stakeholders (i.e., customers and producers)?
3. What is the optimal way to draft input to the COLISEUM database?
4. When is a PR necessary?
5. Can improvements in the assembly and communication of IMD requirements increase timeliness and quality of IMD production?

Findings

1. A standardized and effective acquisition-intelligence governance process is lacking, as is an accepted practice for developing IMD requirements and translating them into intelligence tasks.
2. There appear to be too many stakeholders involved in the IMD task-development process, and their responsibilities are ill-defined.
3. The IMD requirements identification and production development process comprises two distinct phases that vary by service.
4. IMD requirements can generally be binned into three categories: long-term requirements generally associated with an acquisition program; ad hoc requirements that come from combatant commands and operational forces; and requirements that are identified in the annual plan review of IMD requirements.
5. Guidance on PR introduction and processing is obsolete.
6. Some COLISEUM fields could be automated to improve standardization of inputs and ensure better-quality tasking inputs, add precision to tasks, and facilitate movement of tasks between systems. These enhancements would thus improve the timeliness and quality of IMD products.

Recommendations

1. Focus less on the acquisition side of the acquisition-intelligence process and more on the intelligence side, where impact is more likely.
2. Create a demand signal repository by exploring direct electronic connections among the tools and databases currently used to manage IMD issues.
3. Use the upcoming CPI event to seek consensus on the priorities laid out in this report.
4. Consider drafting an IMD manual, similar to the *Joint Capabilities Integration and Development System (JCIDS)* manual,[3] to capture processes and standard operating procedures for IMD professionals.
5. Adopt the RAND-developed process maps.

---

[3] Here and throughout this report, we use the term *JCIDS manual* to refer, as the IMD community does, to the document as it has been incorporated into Chairman of the Joint Chiefs of Staff Instruction 5123.01H, *Charter of the Joint Requirements Oversight Council (JROC) and Implementation of the Joint Capabilities Integration and Development System (JCIDS)*, Washington, D.C., August 31, 2018.

Acknowledgments

We would like to thank Lisa Mazur and her staff at the Acquisition Intelligence Requirements Task Force, especially Lt Col Michael Simons, for their interest in this project; Mike Decker and J. D. Williams for their reviews of the report; Rich Girven for providing the opportunity to undertake this follow-on research and for his review of the report; and Col Andy Souza for providing advice and expertise throughout the project.

Any errors or omissions in this report are the sole responsibility of the authors.

Abbreviations

AIRTF	Acquisition Intelligence Requirements Task Force
AIRViEW	Acquisition Intelligence Requirements Visualization Enterprise Workflows
CCMD	combatant command
CPI	continuous process improvement
CJCSI	Chairman of the Joint Chiefs of Staff Instruction
COLISEUM	Community On-Line Intelligence System for End Users and Managers
DIAP	Defense Intelligence Analysis Program
DoD	U.S. Department of Defense
DoDD	Department of Defense Directive
DoDI	Department of Defense Instruction
DoDIPP	Department of Defense Intelligence Production Program
DSR	demand signal repository
IC	intelligence community
IFC	intelligence functional code

IMARS	Intelligence Mission Data Management, Analysis, and Reporting System
IMD	Intelligence Mission Data
IMDC	Intelligence Mission Data Center
IPC	Intelligence Production Center
JCIDS	Joint Capabilities Integration and Development System
LMDP	Life-Cycle Mission Production Plan
MILDEP	Military Department
NASIC	National Air and Space Intelligence Center
NAVAIR	Naval Air Systems Command
NDRI	RAND National Defense Research Institute
PARCA	Program Assessment and Root Cause Analysis
PR	production requirement
RACI	Responsible, Accountable, Consulted, Informed

CHAPTER ONE

Introduction

Background

This project began on October 5, 2018, when the Office of the Secretary of Defense for Acquisition, Technology and Logistics asked the RAND National Defense Research Institute (NDRI) to examine an effort by the Acquisition Intelligence Requirements Task Force (AIRTF) to improve the understanding of the processes for developing and fulfilling requirements for Intelligence Mission Data (IMD). IMD provides essential data for building system models, developing algorithms, optimizing sensor design, system testing and evaluation, and validating sensor functionality. Programs that depend on IMD to satisfy their operational and system requirements are considered *IMD dependent*.[1] AIRTF hosted a continuous process improvement (CPI) meeting with IMD stakeholders in August 2018 that aimed to identify

---

[1] Defense Intelligence Agency, Defense Technology and Long-Range Analysis Office, *Life-Cycle Mission Data Plan (LMDP): Guidebook and Templates*, Version 3.1, Washington, D.C., April 8, 2014. The *DOD Dictionary of Military and Associated Terms* does not include a definition of IMD (U.S. Department of Defense, *DOD Dictionary of Military and Associated Terms*, Washington, D.C., June 2020). A definition of the term similar but less detailed than the one provided here is included in Department of Defense Directive (DoDD) 5250.01, *Management of Intelligence Mission Data (IMD) in DoD Acquisition*, January 22, 2013, Incorporating Change 1, August 29, 2017. The directive defines *IMD* as "DoD intelligence used for programming platform mission systems in development, testing operations, and sustainment including, but not limited to, the functional areas of signatures, EWIR [electronic warfare integrated reprogramming], OOB [order of battle], C&P [characteristics and performance], and GEOINT [geospatial intelligence]" (p. 13).

and reduce impediments in the process. The meeting, however, did not achieve these goals. Attendees, including representatives from all stakeholder communities, identified the processes by which IMD requirements are currently managed, but the numbers of impediments to the process in all three Military Departments (MILDEPs) were too numerous to resolve at the meeting. AIRTF approached RAND NDRI for assistance in analyzing the data collected at the CPI event and to develop wire frame diagrams (or process maps) of the existing processes employed by the MILDEPs. We took a modified Responsible, Accountable, Consulted, Informed (RACI) approach to assign roles and responsibilities for each aspect of the wire frame diagram to map out roles for each entity involved and reduce confusion.[2] The wire frames aimed to visualize the processes with an eye toward identifying impediments (or pain points) in the processes and provide suggestions for reducing or resolving them to the extent possible. Specifically, AIRTF requested responses to the following questions:

1. Are there policy changes that would reduce inefficiency in the processes?
2. What are the equities of the stakeholders (i.e., customers and producers)?
3. What is the optimal way to draft input to Community On-Line Intelligence System for End Users and Managers (COLISEUM)?[3]
   a. Can input to COLISEUM be automated to reduce effort and error?
   b. Is there preference for automated COLISEUM input?
4. When is a production requirement (PR) necessary?

---

[2] Brett Harned, "How to Clear Project Confusion with a RACI Chart [Template]," Team Gantt webpage, September 16, 2019.

[3] *COLISEUM* is an automated task-management system that provides a mechanism for registering and validating intelligence production requirements across the military intelligence community (IC).

a. Are there business-plan changes that could resolve an ad hoc PR before making it part of the annual plan (e.g., what are urgent needs and how should they be conveyed)?
  b. What are the business rules for ad hoc requests, and can they be improved?
5. What questions can be answered by a more efficient and effective process?
  a. Can the amount of input be reduced and by what order of magnitude?
  b. What are the decision points along the process flow?

Methodology

We applied several methodologies for this research. To develop the wire frames, we used the data provided by AIRTF to map out each step of the process, identify the organizations responsible for each action, and determine the customers for the output. This visualization allowed us to recognize and highlight process impediments. We also used 2014–2018 data to support a study, sponsored by the Office of the Secretary of Defense for Acquisition, Technology, and Logistics' Program Assessment and Root Cause Analysis (PARCA), of intelligence support to acquisition programs. This study developed data on the details of the evolution of the IMD process and gathered insights from interviews of IMD experts. Based on this broad set of data, we suggested revisions to the processes that reduce process steps, ensuring that the output of each successive process was closely linked to the next step in the process.

Separate methodologies were used to address the questions. We undertook a broad review of regulations and instructions that provide governance for the processes. We reviewed departmental, joint, service, and IC guidance. Separately, we conducted a detailed analysis of COLISEUM, the system used to task IC producers for finished intelligence products addressing IMD and other information needs. Based on the process analysis and the deep dive into governance documents and tasking systems, we observed issues that AIRTF might consider to simplify the IMD identification and production process and to use data developed by that process for workflow management and resource-allocation decisions. This could be done by instituting a demand signal repository (DSR).[4]

In Chapter Two, we discuss the analysis involved in developing the wire frame diagrams, impediments in the processes, and possible ways to eliminate or consolidate some actions that might make the process leaner and more effective. In Chapter Three, we address the questions posed by the AIRTF and present our proposed streamlined process maps. In Chapter Four, we discuss observations from the study and make suggestions for AIRTF consideration.

---

[4] Here and throughout the report, we use the term *demand signal repository* to mean "a centralized database that stores, harmonizes and normalizes data attributes and organizes large volumes of demand data . . . for use by decision support technologies. . . . At the enterprise level, DSRs can become the foundation for a comprehensive information architecture strategy, driving an array of demand and supply-related predictive analytic applications and processes" (Gartner, "Demand Signal Repository (DSR)," webpage, undated).

CHAPTER TWO

Current As-Is Processes

We developed acquisition-intelligence process maps for new and sustained programs of the U.S. Air Force, U.S. Army, and U.S. Navy. AIRTF gathered the information on current processes at the August 2018 CPI event, where the group identified too many process impediments to distill easily into useful recommendations. We analyzed these data and developed wire frame diagrams of how the process worked in each MILDEP. To develop the diagrams, we mapped out each step of the process in each of the MILDEPs and identified the organizations responsible for each action and determined the customers for each output.

The visualization allowed us to isolate and highlight process impediments. In the process maps that follow, the column on the far left identifies the *initiator* of the action. The arrow in the second column identifies the task. The organizations in the third column are responsible for acting on the identified task. The arrow in the column on the far right defines the expected output. The final column on the right is the organization receiving the output. Once the steps in the process on the first line are completed, the organization receiving the output initiates work on the tasks associated with the second line. The workflow proceeds in this manner until the stakeholders and responsible parties have worked completely through all steps in the chart.

Mapping the individual steps, the organizations involved in them, and their outputs revealed several seams in the current processes for all the MILDEPs. First, the output of one step does not necessarily link to the input in the subsequent step. Second, the organization receiving the output of the first step is not always the "initiator" of the subsequent step. Third, some steps in the current processes include uncertainties about "initiators," organizations responsible for particular tasks, or organizations receiving the outputs of particular tasks (the *?* in the subsequent figures depict these uncertainties). Fourth, the current processes include such temporary organizations as the AIRTF as "initiators" of some steps (e.g., see Figure 2.2) or organizations responsible for completing a task (e.g., see Figure 2.4, Step 11), the dissolution of which would create another void in the given processes.

After mapping the existing processes, we identified opportunities to conduct some steps concurrently. The revised process flows focused on ensuring that each step informs subsequent steps or supports concurrent steps. Additionally, the revised processes aimed to link the organizations receiving the output of one task with their responsibility to initiate the next task in the subsequent step. Chapter Three presents a discussion of the revised process flows in more detail.

Current Air Force Processes

The Air Force has the most-mature acquisition-intelligence process of all the MILDEPs. Figure 2.1 depicts the existing process for new Air Force programs.

Figure 2.1
Current Process for New Air Force Programs

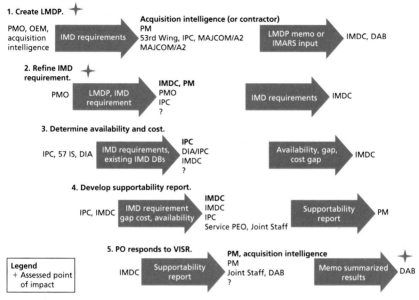

Legend
+ Assessed point of impact

Associated Pain Points
Step 1
1.b. "Programs" requesting "invalid" IMD (processes: IPCs produce IMD, identify gaps)
1.c. Missing IMD-dependent programs (all)
There is no IMD standard that goes to industry baseline.
Step 2
1.d. Justify the determination of PMO choice (reduction in staffing process, percentage of time used to translate or support PMO justification)
1.e. Knowledge of LMDP for PMO (accuracy of requirements)
2.b. PMO/FIO do not identify correct DIEQP/ELNOT. Delay to overall process for RFI (learning curve time, dedicated process analysis)
Step 5
3. DoDI 5000.02, Table 2 (PM regulatory LMDP requirement) is not a decisionmaking document. It has very little value to the decision board (recommendation to change policy to require a VISR) and a PM IMD risk strategy document. The IMD requirements have to be entered to any IMD reporting tool (need to incentivize)

NOTES: ? = unknown organization, not listed in source note; DAB = Defense Acquisition Board; DIA = Defense Intelligence Agency; DIEQP = Defense Intelligence Equipment Index; ELNOT = Electronic Intelligence Notation; FIO = foreign intelligence officer; IMARS = IMD Management, Analysis, and Reporting System; IMDC = Intelligence Mission Data Center; IPC = Intelligence Production Center; IS = Intelligence Squadron; LMDP = Life-Cycle Mission Data Plan; MAJCOM/A2 = major command, Directorate of Intelligence; OEM = original equipment manufacturer; PEO = Program Executive Officer; PM = program manager; PMO = Program Management Office; RFI = request for information; VISR = Validated IMD Supportability Report.

The Air Force process for sustainment programs follows a similar methodology as that for new programs. Requirements flow through the process across and down. Figure 2.2 shows the current process for Air Force sustainment programs.

Current Army Processes

The Army process for new programs follows a similar methodology as those for the Air Force programs. Requirements flow from the top left to the right and down. Figure 2.3 shows the Army process for new programs.

Figure 2.2
Current Process for Air Force Sustainment Programs (Ad Hoc Requirements)

1. Refine requirements for joint (perceived NVA).

2. Determine cost and availability.

NOTES: AIRViEW = Acquisition Intelligence Requirements Visualization Enterprise Workflows; HAF/A2 = Headquarters Air Force, Directorate of Intelligence; MAJCOM = major command; NVA = net value assessment; RO = Requirements Office.

Figure 2.3
Current Process for New Army Programs

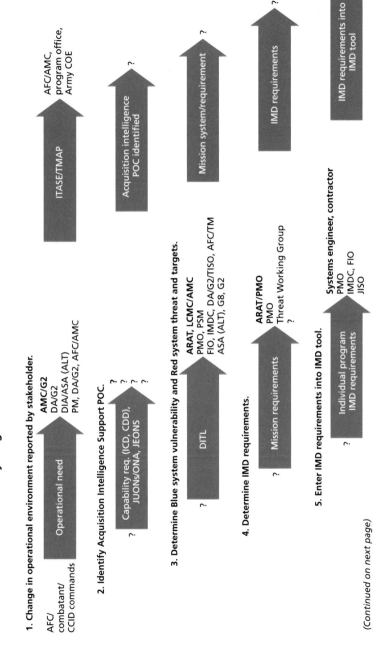

1. Change in operational environment reported by stakeholder.

AFC/
combatant/
CCID commands

Operational need → ITASE/TMAP

AMC/G2
DA/G2
DIA/ASA (ALT)
PM, DA/G2, AFC/AMC

AFC/AMC,
program office,
Army COE

2. Identify Acquisition Intelligence Support POC.

? Capability req. (ICD, CDD),
JUONs/ONA, JEONS
? ? ? ?

Acquisition intelligence
POC identified ?

3. Determine Blue system vulnerability and Red system threat and targets.

? DITL

ARAT, LCMC/AMC
PMO, PSM
FIO, IMDC, DA/G2/TISO, AFC/TM
ASA (ALT), G8, G2

Mission system/requirement ?

4. Determine IMD requirements.

? Mission requirements

ARAT/PMO
PMO
Threat Working Group
?

IMD requirements ?

5. Enter IMD requirements into IMD tool.

? Individual program
IMD requirements

Systems engineer, contractor
PMO
IMDC, FIO
JISO

IMD requirements into
IMD tool ?

(Continued on next page)

Figure 2.3—Continued

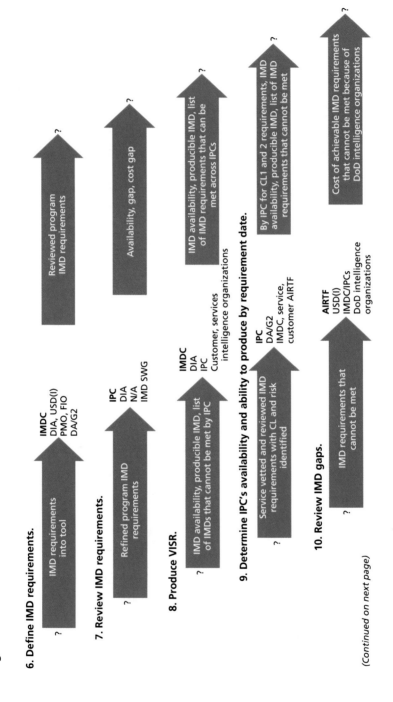

6. Define IMD requirements.

IMD requirements into tool

IMDC
DIA, USD(I)
PMO, FIO
DA/G2

Reviewed program IMD requirements

7. Review IMD requirements.

Refined program IMD requirements

IPC
DIA
N/A
IMD SWG

Availability, gap, cost gap

8. Produce VISR.

IMD availability, producible IMD, list of IMDs that cannot be met by IPC

IMDC
DIA
IPC
Customer, services
intelligence organizations

IMD availability, producible IMD, list of IMD requirements that can be met across IPCs

9. Determine IPC's availability and ability to produce by requirement date.

Service vetted and reviewed IMD requirements with CL and risk identified

IPC
DA/G2
IMDC, service,
customer AIRTF

By IPC for CL1 and 2 requirements, IMD availability, producible IMD, list of IMD requirements that cannot be met

10. Review IMD gaps.

IMD requirements that cannot be met

AIRTF
USD(I)
IMDC/IPCs
DoD intelligence
organizations

Cost of achievable IMD requirements that cannot be met because of DoD intelligence organizations

(Continued on next page)

Figure 2.3—Continued

11. Produce IPC's IMD.

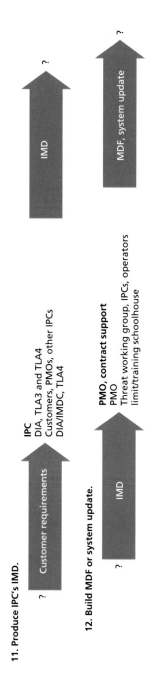

? Customer requirements

IPC
DIA, TLA3 and TLA4
Customers, PMOs, other IPCs
DIA/IMDC, TLA4

12. Build MDF or system update.

? IMD

PMO, contract support
PMO
Threat working group, IPCs, operators
limit/training schoolhouse

IMD ?

MDF, system update ?

NOTES: ? = unknown organization, not listed in source note; A&T = Acquisition and Technology; AFC = Army Futures Command; AMC = Army Materiel Command; ARAT = Army Reprogramming Analysis Team; ASA (ALT) = Assistant Secretary of the Army (Acquisitions, Technology and Logistics); CDD = Capability Development Document; CCID = Coalition Combat Identification; CL = criticality; COE = Corps of Engineers; DA = Department of the Army; DITL = Defense Intelligence Threat Library; DoD = U.S. Department of Defense; FIO = foreign intelligence officer; G2 = Directorate of Intelligence; G8 = U.S. Army Director of Resource Management; ICD = Initial Capabilities Document; ITASE = Integrated Threat Analysis and Simulation Environment; J8 = Joint Chiefs of Staff Director of Force Structure, Resources, and Assessment; JEON = Joint Emergent Operational Need; JISO = Joint Intelligence Support Office; JUON = Joint Urgent Operational Need; LCMC = Life Cycle Mission Center; MDF = mission data file; ONA = Office of Net Assessment; PM = program manager; PMO = Program Management Office; POC = point of contact; PSM = product support manager; SWG = Signals Working Group; TISO = Threat Intelligence Support Office; TLA = technology and long-range analysis; TLA3 = DIA Defense TLA Office for threat coordination; TLA4 = DIA Defense TLA Office for IMD coordination; TM = threat manager; TMAP = Threat Modeling and Analysis Program; USD(I) = Under Secretary of Defense for Intelligence; VISR = Validated IMD Supportability Report.

The Army acquisition-intelligence process for sustainment programs follows the same top-left to bottom-right methodology. Figure 2.4 shows the current process for Army sustainment programs.

Figure 2.4
Current Process for Army Sustainment Programs

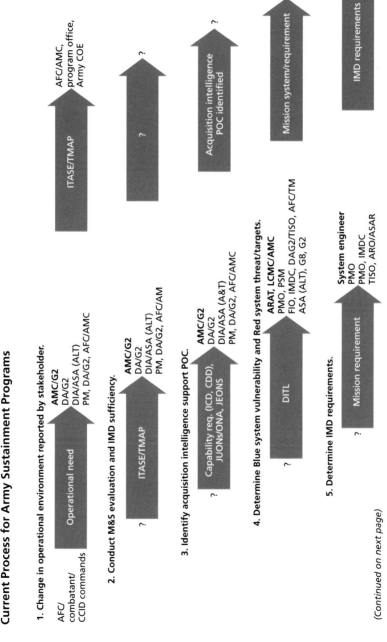

1. Change in operational environment reported by stakeholder.

AFC/
combatant/
CCID commands

AMC/G2
DA/G2
DIA/ASA (ALT)
PM, DA/G2, AFC/AMC

Operational need

AFC/AMC,
program office,
Army COE

ITASE/TMAP

2. Conduct M&S evaluation and IMD sufficiency.

AMC/G2
DA/G2
DIA/ASA (ALT)
PM, DA/G2, AFC/AM

? ITASE/TMAP

?

3. Identify acquisition intelligence support POC.

AMC/G2
DA/G2
DIA/ASA (A&T)
PM, DA/G2, AFC/AMC

? Capability req. (ICD, CDD),
JUONs/ONA, JEONS

Acquisition intelligence
POC identified

?

4. Determine Blue system vulnerability and Red system threat/targets.

ARAT, LCMC/AMC
PMO, PSM
FIO, IMDC, DAG2/TISO, AFC/TM
ASA (ALT), G8, G2

? DITL

Mission system/requirement

?

5. Determine IMD requirements.

System engineer
PMO
PMO, IMDC
TISO, ARO/ASAR

? Mission requirement

IMD requirements

?

(Continued on next page)

Figure 2.4—Continued

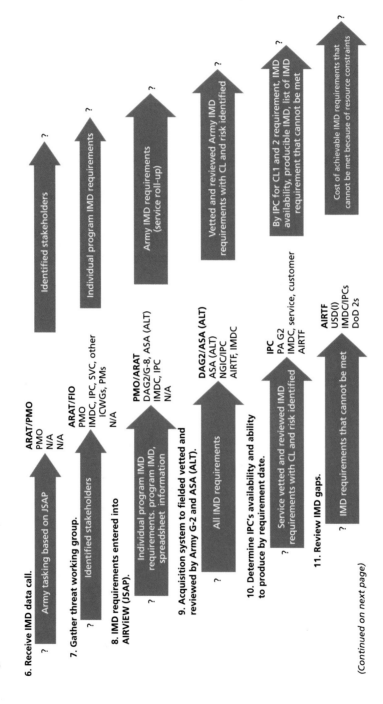

6. Receive IMD data call.

? Army tasking based on JSAP

ARAT/PMO
PMO
N/A
N/A

? Identified stakeholders

7. Gather threat working group.

? Identified stakeholders

ARAT/FIO
PMO
IMDC, IPC, SVC, other
ICWGs, PMs
N/A

? Individual program IMD requirements

8. IMD requirements entered into AIRViEW (JSAP).

? Individual program IMD requirements. program IMD, spreadsheet information

PMO/ARAT
DAG2/G-8, ASA (ALT)
IMDC, IPC
N/A

? Army IMD requirements (service roll-up)

9. Acquisition system to fielded vetted and reviewed by Army G-2 and ASA (ALT).

? All IMD requirements

DAG2/ASA (ALT)
ASA (ALT)
NGIC/IPC
AIRTF, IMDC

? Vetted and reviewed Army IMD requirements with CL and risk identified

10. Determine IPC's availability and ability to produce by requirement date.

? Service vetted and reviewed IMD requirements with CL and risk identified

IPC
PA G2
IMDC, service, customer
AIRTF

? By IPC for CL1 and 2 requirement, IMD availability, producible IMD, list of IMD requirement that cannot be met

11. Review IMD gaps.

? IMD requirements that cannot be met

AIRTF
USD(I)
IMDC/IPCs
DoD 2s

? Cost of achievable IMD requirements that cannot be met because of resource constraints

(Continued on next page)

Figure 2.4—Continued

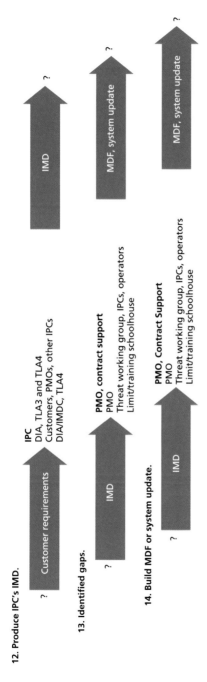

12. Produce IPC's IMD.

? Customer requirements

IPC
DIA, TLA3 and TLA4
Customers, PMOs, other IPCs
DIA/IMDC, TLA4

IMD ?

13. Identified gaps.

? IMD

PMO, contract support
PMO
Threat working group, IPCs, operators
Limit/training schoolhouse

MDF, system update ?

14. Build MDF or system update.

? IMD

PMO, Contract Support
PMO
Threat working group, IPCs, operators
Limit/training schoolhouse

MDF, system update ?

NOTES: ? = unknown organization, not listed in source note; AFC = Army Futures Command; AMC = Army Materiel Command; ARAT = Army Reprogramming Analysis Team; ARO = Army Research Office; ASA (ALT) = Assistant Secretary of the Army (Acquisitions, Technology and Logistics); ASAR = Army Systems Acquisition Review; CCID = Coalition Combat Identification; CDD = Capability Development Document; CL = criticality; COE = Corps of Engineers; DA = Department of the Army; DITL = Defense Intelligence Threat Library; FIO = foreign intelligence officer; G2 = U.S. Army Director of Intelligence; G8 = U.S. Army Director of Resource Management; ICD = Initial Capabilities Document; ICWG = Interface Control Working Group; ITASE = Integrated Threat Analysis and Simulation Environment; JEON = Joint Emergent Operational Need; JSAP = Joint Staff Action Package; JUON = Joint Urgent Operational Need; LCMC = Life Cycle Mission Center; MDF = mission data file; M&S = modeling and simulation; NGIC = National Ground Intelligence Center; ONA = Office of Net Assessment; PM = program manager; PMO = Program Management Office; PSM = product support manager; TISO = Threat Intelligence Support Office; TLA = technology and long-range analysis; TLA3 = DIA Defense TLA Office for threat coordination; TLA4 = DIA Defense TLA Office for IMD coordination; TM = threat manager; TMAP = Threat Modeling and Analysis Program; USD(I) = Under Secretary of Defense for Intelligence.

Current Navy Processes

The Navy processes follow a similar top-left to bottom-right methodology. Figure 2.5 shows the Navy process for new programs.

Navy sustainment programs follow a similar top-left to bottom-right methodology as previously discussed. Figure 2.6 shows the current process for Navy sustainment programs.

Figure 2.5
Current Process for New Navy Programs

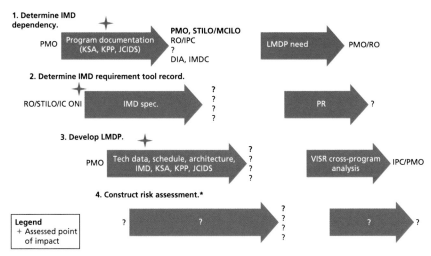

1. Determine IMD dependency.

PMO → Program documentation (KSA, KPP, JCIDS) → PMO, STILO/MCILO RO/IPC ? DIA, IMDC → LMDP need → PMO/RO

2. Determine IMD requirement tool record.

RO/STILO/IC ONI → IMD spec. → ? ? ? ? → PR → ?

3. Develop LMDP.

PMO → Tech data, schedule, architecture, IMD, KSA, KPP, JCIDS → ? ? ? ? → VISR cross-program analysis → IPC/PMO

4. Construct risk assessment.*

? → ? → ? ? ? ? → ? → ?

Legend
+ Assessed point of impact

Associated Pain Points
Steps 1, 2, and 3
Assumption that PMO and RO know what they need or own data rights to the system
(Metrics: number of requirements, number of fields; impacts all)
  a. Assumption that operations community and reprogramming know current and future threat
  b. "Programs" requesting "invalid" IMD (processes: IPCs produce IMD; identify gaps)
  c. Missing IMD-dependent programs (all)
  d. Justify the determination of PMO choice (reduction in staffing process, percent of time used to translate or support PMO justification)
  e. Knowledge of LMDP for PMO (accuracy of requirements)
Steps 3 and 4
3. DoDI 5000.02, Table 2 (PM regulatory LMDP requirements) is not a decisionmaking document. It has very little value to the decision board (recommendation to change policy to require a VISR) and a PM IMD risk strategy document.* The IMD requirements have to be entered to any IMD reporting tool (need to incentivize)
  a. Development of LMDPs is inconsistent across all acquisition programs (processes: IMD production, gaps, AIRViEW entry)

NOTES: * Only Navy current state process requires conducting a risk assessment.
? = unknown organization, not listed in source note; DIA = Defense Intelligence Agency; IC = Intelligence Center; JCIDS = Joint Capabilities Integration and Development System; KPP = key performance parameter; KSA = key system attribute; MCILO = Marine Corps intelligence liaison officer; ONI = Office of Naval Intelligence; PMO = Program Management Office; RO = requirements officer; STILO = science and technology intelligence liaison officer; VISR = Validated IMD Supportability Report.

Navy sustainment programs follow a similar top-left to bottom-right methodology as previously discussed. Figure 2.6 shows the current process for Navy sustainment programs.

Figure 2.6
Current Process for Navy Sustainment Programs

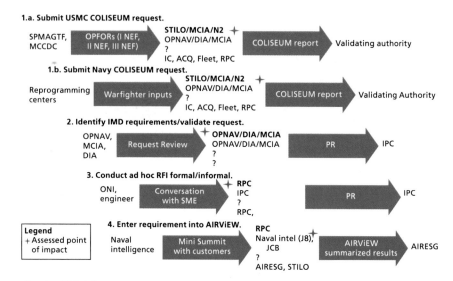

Associated Pain Points
Step 1
4. Work requirements by EWIR, C&P, signatures, OB, M&S (no object basis, IPC production shifting to object-based production)
   a. No linkage between threat updates and IMD; new/retired and VOLT to prioritize list; DPS/AORs
Step 2
11. There is no IMD standard that goes to industry baseline
Steps 1, 2, and 4
2. Capturing IMD requirements in multiple tool (entering requirements by hand)
   a. (AIRViEW) No defined process, no collective resource/expertise. Metrics: review boards/process boards.
   b. PMO/FIO don't identify correct DIEQP/ELNOT. Delay to overall process for RFI (learning curve time, dedicated process analysis)
   c. Transfer of IMD requirements into AIRViEW, though AIRViEW does not drive IPC production plans, LMDP construction, etc.
Steps 1, 2 and 3
5. Difficult to identify what requirements are already slated for production. Therefore, annual data calls result in the same work as previously done (in prior fiscal years) (Recommendation to add an effective feedback process that eases the generation process.)
   a. Lack of visibility/transparency of validity of requirements across the community
   b. Lack of visibility for programs to see other programs submission (no cross program priority/analysis)
   c. Linking OPINTEL to S&T intelligence for validation of requirements (threat analysis)
   d. Under current processes, NGIC could assess its ability to satisfy IMD requirements for a single program multiple times in one year

(Continued on next page)

Figure 2.6—Continued

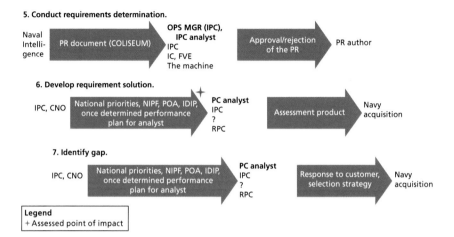

Legend
+ Assessed point of impact

Associated Pain Points
Step 6
8. Prioritization process is arbitrary. Too many elements to prioritize 1 to *N*, but four categories invite "gaming" and do not result in transmission of priorities to IPCs
   a. Lack of fidelity of inter-NIPF categories
   b. Lack of criteria and steps to prioritize between requirements with same CL

NOTES: ? = unknown organization, not listed in source note; ACQ = acquisition; AIRESG = Acquisition Intelligence Requirements Executive Steering Group; AOR = area of responsibility; CL = criticality; CNO = Chief of Naval Operations; C&P = characteristics and performance; DIA = Defense Intelligence Agency; DIEQP = Defense Intelligence Equipment Index; DPS = Defense Priorities System; ELNOT = Electronic Intelligence Notation; EWIR = Electronic Warfare Integrated Reprogramming; FVE = Five Eyes alliance; IDIP = integrated defense intelligence priorities; J8 = Joint Staff, Director of Force Structure, Resources, and Assessment; JCB = Joint Capabilities Board; M&S = modeling and simulation; MCCDC = Marine Corps Combat Development Command; MCIA = Marine Corps Intelligence Activity; N2 = U.S. Navy Directorate of Intelligence; NEF = Naval Expeditionary Force; NIPF = National Intelligence Priorities Framework; OB = order of battle; ONI = Office of Naval Intelligence; OPINTEL = operational intelligence; OPFOR = operating force; OPNAV = Office of the Chief of Naval Operations; POA = program of analysis; RFI = request for information; RPC = Regional Processing Center; S&T = science and technology; SME = subject-matter expert; SPMAGTF = Special Purpose Marine Air-Ground Task Force; STILO = science and technology intelligence liaison officer; USMC = U.S. Marine Corps.

CHAPTER THREE

Governance of Intelligence Mission Data Activities: Processes and Tools

Developing IMD requirements is a complex undertaking that involves coordination and collaboration among three separate and culturally different communities: requirements, acquisition, and intelligence. Previous RAND research about how these communities interact, specifically on how intelligence staff provide threat intelligence to program managers and others and IMD support to requirements and acquisition offices, concluded that a fundamental problem in the process was poor or insufficient communication.[1] Each of the three communities speaks a different language—for example, *requirement* means vastly different things to staff in each community, and there is too little direct communication between intelligence support officers and requirements and acquisition officers. Our research also revealed that processes connecting these three communities do not benefit from effective governance in the form of regulations and instructions.[2] Practices that connect the communities exist, but they differ significantly by organization or service. Nonstandard practices, coupled with various levels of expertise of the staff involved in the

---

[1] Interviews with requirements, acquisition, and intelligence personnel, 2014–2015. We conducted these interviews to support an effort by PARCA to identify impediments in the IC's efforts to provide threat intelligence to acquisition programs. The results of these interviews were informally provided to PARCA but were not published.

[2] Interviews with requirements, acquisition, and intelligence personnel, 2014–2015.

process, likely result in output that differs in content and quality, even if it appears to be similar.

To improve our understanding of the various processes, we sought to identify and review regulations and instructions providing guidance to IMD-related processes. We identified and reviewed 29 relevant policy and governance documents (see Table 3.1).

The plethora of departmental and service documents does not, in its totality, provide processes or standards that can be used by stakeholders who must identify IMD requirements and ensure that they are communicated to the appropriate intelligence organization for action. The inefficiency in this process led AIRTF to raise a series of questions:

1. Are there policy changes that would reduce inefficiency in the processes?
2. What are the equities of the stakeholders (i.e., customers and producers)?
3. What is the optimal way to draft input to COLISEUM?
   a. Can input to COLISEUM be automated to reduce effort and error?
   b. Is there preference for automated COLISEUM input?
4. When is a PR necessary?
   a. How does COLISEUM work?
   b. Are there business plan changes that could resolve an ad hoc PR before making it part of the annual plan (e.g., what are urgent needs and how should they be conveyed)?
   c. What are the business rules for ad hoc requests, and can they be improved?
5. Can improvements in the assembly and communication of IMD requirements increase timeliness and quality of IMD production?
   a. Can the amount of input be reduced and by what order of magnitude?
   b. Can a standardized workflow process identifying "owners" at each step facilitate smoother flow of IMD requirements to producers?

We address these questions in the next sections.

Table 3.1
Relevant Documents Identified

Document	Title
Air Force Instruction 10-703	*Electronic Warfare (EW) Integrated Reprogramming*
Air Force Instruction 14-111	*Intelligence Support to the Air Force Acquisition Life-Cycle (rescinded)*
Army Regulation 381-11	*Intelligence Support to Capability Development*
Better Buying Power 3.0	*Better Buying Power 3.0: Achieving Dominant Capabilities Through Technical Excellence and Innovation*
Chairman of the Joint Chiefs of Staff Instruction (CJCSI) 3901.01D	*Requirements for Geospatial Information and Services*
CJCSI 3000	Draft of IMD prioritization
CJCSI 3170.01a	*Joint Capabilities Integration and Development System (JCIDS)*
CJCSI 3210.03	*Joint Electronic Warfare Policy*
CJCSI 3320.01D	*Joint Electromagnetic Spectrum Operations (JEMSO)*
CJCSI 5123.01H	*Charter of the Joint Requirements Oversight Council (JROC) and Implementation of the Joint Capabilities Integration and Development System (JCIDS)*
CJCSI 6212.01F	*NET Ready Key Performance Parameter (NR KPP)*
COLISEUM	*Community On-Line System for End Users and Managers*
Defense Acquisition Guidebook	*Defense Acquisition Guidebook*
Defense Intelligence Analysis Program (DIAP)	DIAP
DoD-0000-151C-98	*Department of Defense Intelligence Production Program: Requirements Management*
Department of Defense Directive (DoDD) 3222.04	*Electronic Warfare (EW) Policy*
DoDD 5250.01	*Management of Intelligence Mission Data (IMD) in DoD Acquisition*
Department of Defense Instruction (DoDI) 5000.02T	*Operation of the Defense Acquisition System*

Table 3.1—Continued

Document	Title
DoDI 5000.002	*Defense Intelligence Threat Support for Major Defense Acquisition Programs*[b]
DoDI 5000.56	*Programming Geospatial-Intelligence (GEOINT), Geospatial Information and Services (GI&S), and Geodesy Requirements for Developing Systems*
Department of the Navy Regulation 8311.1	*Support to Acquisition*[b]
GAO-17-10	*Defense Intelligence: Additional Steps Could Better Integrate Intelligence Input into DOD's Acquisition of Major Weapon Systems*
Intelligence Mission Data Center guidebook	*Life-Cycle Mission Data Plan (LMDP) Guidebook and Templates*
Intelligence Mission Data Cost Methodology Guidebook	*Intelligence Mission Data Cost Methodology Guidebook*
JCIDS manual[a]	*Manual for the Operation of the Joint Capabilities Integration and Development System*
MARCORSYSCOM Acquisition Guidebook (MAG) 5000.3B	*Implementation of Marine Corps Systems Command Acquisition Tools*
National Air and Space Intelligence Center (NASIC) Instruction 10-102	Issue Manager Instructions
OPNAVINST 3811.1F	*Threat Support to the Defense Acquisition System*
OPNAVINST 3880.6A	*Scientific and Technical Intelligence Liaison Officer (STILO) Program and Intelligence Support for the Naval Research, Development, Test and Evaluation, and Acquisition Communities*

[a] Throughout this report, we use the term *JCIDS manual* to refer, as the IMD community does, to that document as it has been incorporated into Chairman of the Joint Chiefs of Staff Instruction 5123.01H, *Charter of the Joint Requirements Oversight Council (JROC) and Implementation of the Joint Capabilities Integration and Development System (JCIDS)*, Washington, D.C., August 31, 2018.

[b] This document has been rescinded since the writing of this report.

Are There Policy Changes That Would Reduce Inefficiency in the Processes?

We surveyed policy and governance documents with the goal of identifying those that provide general and specific guidance on IMD requirement identification and production processes. Guidance documents include U.S. Department of Defense (DoD) and Joint Chiefs of Staff regulations and instructions, DIA and service regulations and instructions, and training documents that provide some indication of production processes. In addition to the regulations and instructions we surveyed, we reviewed documentation associated with COLISEUM to try to identify how production requirements are produced, validated, tasked, and completed. COLISEUM is the IC's official tasking system by which an IC organization can task another for intelligence production.[3]

Overall, the instructions and regulations do not provide specific or sufficient guidance on how IMD requirements are to be processed once they are identified. The IMD requirement identification process varies by service and by whether the requirement is long-term, ad hoc, or a need identified in the annual plan. For long-term requirements, JCIDS requires programs to complete an LMDP.[4]

We canvassed the services to determine if there were any service-specific regulations, instructions, or other guidance documents specific to IMD. The Air Force uses Air Force Intelligence– and NASIC-level documents that provide some guidance, but they are not specific to IMD. The Army and Navy have no official guidance documents about IMD production.

COLISEUM-related documentation includes the manual used to train new COLISEUM users dated June 2016 and a 1998 document that provides detailed guidance about how intelligence requirements should

---

[3]   The DIAP website, accessed on closed networks on October 28, 2018, identifies COLISEUM as the defense intelligence enterprise's interagency tasking vehicle.

[4]   Joint Capabilities Integration and Development System Manual, *Manual for the Operation of the Joint Capabilities Integration and Development System (JCIDS)*, Appendix I, Enclosure D, p. D-I-10. Note that a newer version of this manual was circulated in 2018.

be processed in the tasking system.[5] This program was restructured in 2004 into the DIAP, which provides guidance sanctioned by the Defense Intelligence Enterprise about production "lanes in the road" for all defense intelligence producers.[6] Although COLISEUM remains the tool by which one organization tasks another for production, DIAP policies differ considerably from those of the DoDIPP. DoDIPP, the production program that preceded DIAP, was established in 1995 and designed to coordinate defense intelligence production by integrating the resources of the entire military IC through the designation of primary and collaborative production responsibilities to assigned centers of excellence. COLISEUM provides the key mechanism for articulating and tracking production requirements across all production centers.[7] The COLISEUM document has not been updated since 1998 and, because of its age and obsolescence, the guidance provided may no longer be authoritative; however, some organizations may choose to follow it in the absence of other direction.[8] This document also provides detailed guidance about the responsibilities of organizations that send tasks into COLISEUM. Specifically, organizations initiating a production requirement in the system are required to "validate" the requirement by ascertaining that there is no collected intelligence that answers the requirement.

---

[5]   The 1998 document was developed to support the then-DIA intelligence production management effort called the *Department of Defense Intelligence Production Program (DoDIPP)*.

[6]   Per the DIAP website.

[7]   In 2004, the DIAP replaced DoDIPP, a highly centralized analytic production program, with a decentralized program that allowed each member to manage analysis for its own organizations and consumers.

[8]   The *Department of Defense Intelligence Production Program: Requirements Management* document, dated November 1998 and not available to the general public, is likely obsolete because it has not been updated or replaced since the publication date. It contains useful definitions that likely remain current. The document defines a *production requirement* as "the term used to describe an RFI that cannot be met by available finished intelligence and that has been validated and assigned to a production center for production" (DoD, *Department of Defense Intelligence Production Program: Requirements Management*, Washington, D.C., November 1998, Not available to the general public).

What Are the Equities of the Stakeholders (i.e., Customers and Producers)?

A closer review of IMD requirements revealed that they can be binned into three categories: (1) long-term requirements generally associated with an acquisition program, (2) ad hoc requirements not derived from an acquisition program's LMDP or needs that come from combatant commands (CCMDs) and operational forces, and (3) requirements that are identified in the annual plan review of IMD requirements. Each category has different processes for requirement validation and tasking. Moreover, it appears that each service has different approaches to the three categories of requirements further complicating the situation. The three types of IMD requirements differ markedly; although they all identify IMD requirements, the requirements are developed for specific purposes by each community. The way the requirements are identified is specific to that community's culture, and the way the tasks are articulated does not mean the tasks are actionable by the IC.

Another way to look at this process is through a demand-supply framework, in which acquisition and operational consumers represent the demand signal, while intelligence provides the supply.

The Demand Signal

In the first, or *demand signal*, portion of the process, identification and refinement of the IMD requirements are generally conducted with the acquisition and operational community (where programs and operators work with intelligence support officers or intelligence liaison officers to characterize the requirement).

The acquisition community's demand signal is captured in the LMDP, which articulates IMD requirements for equipment still in the acquisition process. Required by DoDD 5250.01 and the JCIDS process, the LMDP is defined as the "program manager's plan for how the program manager and other organizations will address specific program needs for IMD. It contains the results of IMD planning and spans the entire lifecycle of an IMD-dependent acquisition program." The LMDP is an acquisition document designed to support the program manager and provides a basis for program planning. The document identifies IMD requirements, but it is not "actionable" in the intelligence sense, because the precise IMD requirements are not sufficiently detailed to become intelligence production tasks without additional work to specify the precise questions and to direct those questions to specific intelligence producers. A simple search of COLISEUM identified 44 LMDPs that have been validated as intelligence production requirements.

The operational community's demand signal for intelligence is of a more immediate and specific nature. Ad hoc IMD requirements, typically initiated by operators, reach the IC in a different and distinct way. According to information from the IMDC, most ad hoc requests enter the system from the reprogramming centers and include a limited number of individual data requests. These requirements are generally initiated by operational forces through CCMDs or service operational elements. Additionally, these requirements are characterized as being specific and having an indication when a response is required.

The Supply Side

The second, or *supply side*, process is conducted within the IC. Intelligence stakeholders face several issues in responding to production tasks resulting from the identification of IMD requirements. IMD production requests come in different forms; some PRs contain large numbers of discrete requests for data, while other PRs contain only a few. Identifying the priority in which these tasks are completed can be complicated and contentious, especially if the requestor has not provided specific guidance indicating when the data are required. Another prioritization complication concerns the relative seniority or importance of the consumer; do more-senior organizations or customers get priority over lower-level consumers, or does the joint staff or a CCMD get higher priority than a program office? Priority in addressing PRs may not be informed by good information about when responses are required, and intelligence production efforts fail if data reach a consumer too late to be useful.

Where PRs are registered is also unclear. The basic assumption is that IMD-related PRs are tasked through COLISEUM, but this assumption is likely incorrect; anecdotal data suggest that many requirements are passed from consumers to intelligence production elements via email or phone, and responses are provided directly and are not processed through any tasking system. This informal information-acquisition mechanism suggests that users find the system too inefficient or burdensome to provide timely responses to requests or that they are not confident that a request put into the system will provide a product in return. We can access and study requirements codified in COLISEUM, but we have no way to enumerate and assess tasks that are not processed through this or other tasking systems.

The IMDC states the importance of the IMD planning process. The following potential benefits are noted:

- Early intelligence planning reduces program costs and risk by enabling the IC to better plan, prioritize and resource future IMD requirements.
- Identification of IMD requirements enables justification of non-program resources to be applied to areas that have cross-program or cross-service overlap.
- Drives standardization of IMD definitions, metadata, and customer interfaces with the end goal of automated data dissemination.
- Analysis of IMD gaps and program risk can influence both acquisition and intelligence community tool/technology development with sufficient time to impact the program.[9]

Enumeration of these benefits suggests that a closer look at DoDD 5250.01 and the included authorities might uncover unused authorities that could be used to empower efforts to ameliorate IMD identification and production problems. For instance, standardization of IMD metadata and customer interfaces alone would likely reduce confusion between organizations and reduce the amount of time consumed during coordination between tasking and tasked organizations as they attempt to develop a list of requirements that

---

[9]   Defense Acquisition University, "Program Management: DAU Sponsored Documents," webpage ("Benefits of DoDD 5250.01 & IMD Planning Process for the Acquisition Community [AC]"), June 1, 2017.

both represent actual intelligence needs but could also be absorbed by intelligence producers as actionable tasks.

What Is the Optimal Way to Draft Input to COLISEUM?

Previous RAND research of COLISEUM and other IC tasking systems reveals that poorly written requirements are often the source of delays in production and that the most-effective inputs to COLISEUM have a clear description of the task to ensure that the request moves to the proper analytic center for immediate action.[10] This finding was echoed in—and the process impediments identified during—the CPI meeting. An initial review of IMD-related requirements contained in COLISEUM suggests that this problem may currently impede the IMD production process, especially for LMDP-related production as noted earlier. A sampling of those documents showed that the LMDP document had been appended to the COLISEUM task or had been cut and pasted into the COLISEUM document. In some cases, the LMDP description of the task was inadequate to spark intelligence production; LMDPs are not actionable intelligence documents—and are not meant to be. We did not have sufficient time to identify and review individual COLISEUM tasks for products, so it is not clear if these tasks are similarly difficult for an IPC to use as a basis for production.

In addition to the substantive characteristics of the PR, the administrative element of the task is also important. The PR must accurately capture which production centers are responsible for the requirement; this means that the correct intelligence functional code (IFC) must be accurately selected so that the task moves to the production center responsible for that topic as identified in the DIAP. In the case of a large requirement involving different producers, the task will need to be "split" (see explanation later in this chapter). One production center, however, will need to be identified as the integrator. Other codes embedded in the COLISEUM worksheet, such as the equipment code or the electronic intelligence notation code, must also

---

[10] Bradley Knopp, unpublished RAND Corporation research, 2017.

be completed accurately to ensure data are developed and stored in the appropriate databases so other users can access it. These codes also play a role in the validation process, in part to avoid task duplication. Appending appropriate IFC and equipment codes requires a level of expertise that may not always be achieved in the COLISEUM tasking process; RAND research suggests that analysts do not always have COLISEUM accounts and training but depend on administrative support staff who are likely not substantive subject-matter experts to perform this task.[11]

Finally, COLISEUM policy requires that PRs be revalidated annually to ensure the request remains current. This annual revalidation requirement provides the opportunity for consumers and intelligence producers to refresh the statement of requirements and the timelines in which production is needed.

Can Input to COLISEUM Be Automated to Reduce Effort and Error?
The inclusion of some COLISEUM fields can be automated. Much of the demographic data (e.g., requestor, program name, task classification, points of contact) could be transferred to COLISEUM if the appropriate database links and application program interfaces were in place. Tasks in their native environment would have to include as many of the same fields as those in COLISEUM to make this effort worthwhile. Automating population of other data fields, particularly IFC codes, would be difficult, because COLISEUM uses a unique set of IFC codes. For those codes that do not lend themselves to automation, one way to improve accuracy in completing them would be to use pull-down menus instead of user-entered text, because pull-down menus would eliminate variations in data entry by standardizing the input. COLISEUM already makes extensive use of pull-down menus to facilitate and standardize data entry.

One complication in this transfer of data, however, would be ensuring that the data elements to be exchanged are entered using the same nomenclature and conventions. This could be difficult with COLISEUM because of the specialized naming conventions used in

---

[11] Bradley Knopp, unpublished RAND Corporation research, 2017.

the system to identify tasking elements, producers, and consumers. A second potential complication is that exchanging data between or among databases assumes the data in each are authoritative. This assumption, however, may be inaccurate.

Is There Preference for Automated COLISEUM Input?

We could not determine an answer to this question without interviewing users. In a separate RAND study, IC producers expressed frustration with COLISEUM in general but were more frustrated with the requirement to duplicate tasks in two or three different systems.[12] During a workshop held to support another RAND project, intelligence analysts supporting a program office explained that they were required to enter tasks into COLISEUM, the IMARS, and AIRViEW.[13] COLISEUM was identified as the preferred system, because it led to receipt of an intelligence product that responded directly to their needs.

When Is a Production Requirement Necessary?

There is little reference in documentation concerning when the services, commands, or acquisition programs initiate and validate intelligence production requirements for threat intelligence and IMD. COLISEUM guidance requires that any organization tasking for intelligence production "validate" the requirement to ensure that current databases do not hold the necessary information and to ascertain whether other tasks seeking the same information exist. The most extensive definition of this task is contained in COLISEUM, which includes information that visually depicts the PR process as it is envisaged to operate (see Figure 3.1).

---

[12] Interview with Naval Air Systems Command (NAVAIR) scientific and technical intelligence liaison officer, June 20, 2018.

[13] Interview with NAVAIR scientific and technical intelligence liaison officer, June 20, 2018.

Figure 3.1
COLISEUM Production Requirement Process

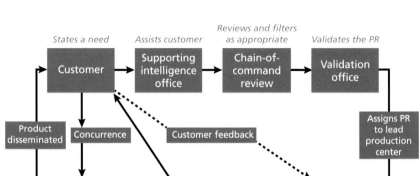

With COLISEUM access, any user can monitor each step of the process.

SOURCE: COLISEUM.

COLISEUM outlines specific customer responsibilities to

- conduct a reasonable search of available sources for the information
- provide an accurate definition and purpose of intelligence needs
- solicit assistance from organic or supporting intelligence elements to formulate a well-defined requirement
- enter the request into COLISEUM if desired or request the supporting intelligence office to enter it
- communicate with assigned production center when necessary to further define PR
- respond to production center proposal within five days or concurrence will be assumed
- provide customer feedback.[14]

14 DoD, 1998, p. 2.

The validation process puts significant emphasis on the original tasking organization for researching existing intelligence for answers and to ensure that the requirement has not been duplicated elsewhere. It is not clear to us that this task is being fulfilled, because we were unable to research it in more detail in the time allotted.

How Does COLISEUM Work?

COLISEUM has more than 21,000 registered users from more than 2,600 organizations.[15] In addition to IC and CCMD users, the list of registered organizations includes operational and tactical-level units of the services and other elements of the national security community. Those with accounts in COLISEUM have certain authorities to use the system to task IC elements for production. COLISEUM policy emphasizes that the system is designed to be used to move production tasks *between* IC production centers, not for internal tasks within an organization. Those with COLISEUM system access are in many cases administrative staff who manage production organization tasks. A previous review of COLISEUM concluded that one aspect of the COLISEUM "problem" is that users are not generally substantive experts in the topics they are asked to manage, so the "translation" of a substantive task into the COLISEUM format may be incomplete or inaccurate.

The sheer number of organizations that can enter a task into COLISEUM, the relative paucity of detailed guidance or governance on how PRs are to arrive at the point of tasking, and the lack of expertise of individuals entering PRs into the system all but ensure differences in the quality of the preceding validation process and in how the requirement is characterized in the incoming PR. Additionally and worth repeating, there is a high likelihood that many tasks in COLISEUM are duplicated.

---

[15] Bradley Knopp, unpublished RAND Corporation research, 2017.

COLISEUM Production Requirement Validation Process

DIA, each service, and the CCMD have COLISEUM PR validation offices that have the following responsibilities:[16]

- Ensure customer needs do not duplicate existing requirements.
- Ensure that the requirement cannot be readily satisfied by existing information.
- Review the requirement for appropriateness, completeness, and scope. If the requirement is not written in a clear and concise manner, the validation office has the authority to return the request to the customer or supporting intelligence office for further clarification.
- Reject requirements that are inappropriate, such as requests for intelligence information that is not substantive.
- Split a requirement into multiple requirements if the action would better serve the customer and the customer agrees to it.
- Select all appropriate geographic and IFCs for the requirement.
- Assign the requirement to the lead production centers.
- Coordinate all requirements that include release of intelligence to a foreign government with the validation office's foreign disclosure office. Enter any guidance received into the requirement prior to assignment to a production center. The production center's foreign disclosure office must approve the release of the product.
- Close the requirement after customer feedback is obtained and no further action is required or after 30 days have passed since dissemination, whichever occurs first. The customer or supporting intelligence office can act to close the requirement as well.
- Accomplish revalidation of all active requirements annually based on the date of the original validation.

Splitting a Production Requirement

PRs, especially those that include multiple questions, may not be completed by a single IPC. In this case, the COLISEUM validation

---

[16] DoD, 1998, p. 3.

office is required to split the tasks that are directed to different producers. Splitting the task is guided by specific production responsibilities accepted by participating intelligence organizations, known as "lanes in the road," identified in the DIAP. The validator will assign a single IPC to integrate the response to a task. This decision is generally based on the IPC, which has the preponderance of requirements. The need to split tasks is another aspect of the process in which inefficiencies may occur and where time is spent managing the process rather than on analysis. Although we did not have sufficient time or resources to research this area of the process in detail, we assess that there are sufficient data to do so. COLISEUM records include extensive data related to the splitting decision and the communication between production elements involved in any split-production request. Analysis of a select number of these records could identify systemic problems that could be ameliorated or eliminated with new or revised policies.

Post–Production Requirement Validation Processes

According to COLISEUM, "validated" PRs emerging from originating organizations undergo additional time-consuming coordination activities once they reach the COLISEUM office.[17] These activities provide for a coordinating discussion between the ultimate consumer, the COLISEUM office, and the producer about the broad details of the product to be delivered. Timelines associated with this activity are shown in Table 3.2.

We identified these timelines that govern the process in the documentation we reviewed. These timelines identify how long validation offices *at any level* have to process a requirement. Note that the first two steps, between the customer and the validating office, can take up to ten working days. Additional communication between the customer and the producer, according to this guidance, is scheduled at 20-day intervals until the task is complete. We had neither the time nor the budget to confirm whether these timelines are observed, but this could be accomplished through analysis of IMD-related tasks in COLISEUM.

---

[17] DoD, 1998, p. 5.

Table 3.2
COLISEUM Timelines

Action	Time Allowed
Registration of requirement	As soon as possible after receiving the need from customer
Chain of command review	Five working days or 10% of the time prior to suspense, whichever is less
Validation	Five working days or 10% of the time prior to suspense, whichever is less
Interim response	20 working days or 10% of the time prior to suspense, whichever is less
Follow-up response	20 working days or 10% of the time prior to suspense, whichever is less
Proposed product response	20 working days or 10% of the time prior to suspense, whichever is less
Customer's initial response to proposal	Five working days or 10% of the time prior to suspense, whichever is less

SOURCE: COLISEUM.

Are There Business-Plan Changes That Could Resolve an Ad Hoc Production Requirement Before Making It Part of the Annual Plan (e.g., What Are Urgent Needs and How Should They Be Conveyed?)

A concept discussed in more-recent academic and professional studies of workflow and output analysis—supply-chain management analysis—is *demand signal repository*.[18] The term has developed in recent years as data collection and storage have increased and the ability to analyze very large volumes of data has become more sophisticated. There is no officially recognized definition of the term, but one comprehensive definition is offered by Gartner, Inc.:

> The demand signal repository (DSR) is a centralized database that stores, harmonizes and normalizes data attributes and organizes large volumes of demand data . . . for use by decision support technologies. . . . At the enterprise level, DSRs can become the foundation for a comprehensive information architecture strategy,

---

[18] Bradley Knopp, unpublished RAND Corporation research, 2017.

driving an array of demand and supply-related predictive analytic applications and processes.[19]

Understanding the comprehensive demand signal for IMD products, one that includes both planned and ad hoc requirements, would help production managers ascertain and prioritize tasks to ensure focus on the highest priority requirements, align personnel and expertise to priority tasks, avoid duplication, and establish a basis for recurring assessments of the effectiveness of the intelligence support to customers based on actual customer requirements. Understanding the demand signal would be foundational to any effort to assess fulfillment of IMD requirements and to establish performance metrics and measures of effectiveness to continuously gauge customer-satisfaction efforts.

If the requirement-validation process is functioning properly, there should be little to no duplication of effort for products that have been completed or previously tasked. The validation effort could be significantly enhanced if validators had access to all tasking systems containing requests for IMD or if there was a single repository for IMD requirements, such as IMARS. This latter capability is currently being developed in the private sector to manage service provision and product manufacturing.[20] There is no demand-signal repository-like capability in the IC for managing intelligence tasks. The creation of semistructured demand signal repository databases and populating them specifically to oversee complex production processes involving distributed producers that provide inputs to common tasks would likely go a long way to resolving many of the issues that exist.

What Are the Business Rules for Ad Hoc Requests, and Can They Be Improved?

Limited time and resources prevented us from reviewing this question in any detail. Information gathered in previous research and a short interview with IMDC staff suggest that there are no unique

---

[19] Gartner, "Gartner Glossary: Demand Signal Repository (DSR)," website, undated.

[20] Bradley Knopp, unpublished RAND Corporation research, 2017.

business rules for ad hoc requests. A limited search of COLISEUM revealed the presence of only a few such tasks; some of the tasks identified were "after-the-fact" taskers put into the system to codify an already-completed action. Given the large numbers of these tasks, additional review of processes with the IMDC and the reprogramming labs would likely be enlightening. Analysis of the current processes using actual tasking data might reveal insights that could reduce impediments and improve overall effectiveness.

Can Improvements in the Assembly and Communication of Intelligence Mission Data Requirements Improve Timeliness and Quality of Intelligence Mission Data Production?

The apparent multiplicity of methods by which IMD needs are identified, validated, and tasked makes it difficult to answer this question. Internal service processes develop around specific cultures and are less available to review or modify. Processes that govern the movement of an IMD task through the intelligence production process should be more malleable, although the numbers of intelligence stakeholders and the multiplicity of production centers involved in development of most finished intelligence products makes efficiency a harder goal to achieve. Analysis of the CPI data and the process wire frames we developed show that the numbers of stakeholders in the IMD task-development process are large and their responsibilities ill-defined. It is unclear to us what responsibilities stakeholders in the process with advisory, coordinating, or information access have. The absence of any identifiable governance document suggests that these responsibilities may be defined differently by different programs and MILDEPs and that the definition of responsibilities may change over time as individual players rotate through the system.

Our research did not discover any guidance on standard action timelines. The timelines identified earlier, which were extracted from COLISEUM, suggest that the initial part of the process—receiving and validating a PR—can take up to 30 days. Although this may be appropriate for a long-term requirement, such as those identified in LMDPs, it is unlikely that operational consumers could or would accept this latency.

Can the Amount of Input Be Reduced, and By What Order of Magnitude?

For program offices developing the LMDP, this task must involve internal and external stakeholders. Program engineers and program intelligence support personnel work together to identify the requirements, then intelligence support officers research the requirements to determine if new production is required. Once this level of work is completed, the requirement begins to move through the system. This process appears to be different in each service. In the Air Force, the task moves from the program office into intelligence channels, where it is validated against IPC holdings and consolidated with other IMD requirements. Once this level of validation is complete and there is certainty about new production by an intelligence organization other than that in the Air Force is required, it moves to COLISEUM. The processes for the Navy and Army are less clear. A discussion with NAVAIR science and technical intelligence liaison officers revealed that IMD requirements for the programs under their auspices are all funneled through a single intelligence support office that provides quality control to ensure that tasks are actionable, not duplicative, and reasonable in terms of intelligence sought over a specific timeline. This process is not currently captured in governance documents. The Army does not appear to have a similar process, and limited time and funding prevented us from further researching this process.

Input to task development is complex, and issues arise from the differing perspectives of the stakeholders. Programs and operational units are interested in the data, not where it originates. The LMDP is a document required by the JCIDS process, and program managers often place more importance on completing the document than on its content. Intelligence liaison officers and COLISEUM validators turn those needs into actionable intelligence tasks, but validation and tasking efforts are only as good as the requirement received. The level of substantive expertise on the part of intelligence liaison officers and COLISEUM validators is also a critical factor because additional input may sometimes be necessary to successfully translate an operational requirement into an actionable intelligence task. The absence of high-level service policies for how this flow should occur and the apparent differences among the stakeholders in how tasks are identified, validated, and communicated—even in a service—means that there are no standards to be observed by widely dispersed intelligence customers and intelligence support personnel. This significantly complicates the process of digesting requirements, deconflicting requirements, and ensuring that requirements are not duplicated. This put a significant burden on intelligence liaison officers who mostly do the tasking and COLISEUM validators who direct the tasks to appropriate IPCs to do this work.

Can a Standardized Workflow Process Identifying "Owners" at Each Step Facilitate Smoother Flow of Intelligence Mission Data Requirements to Producers?

In an effort to identify and eliminate confusion in the workflows, we revised the current process flows to attempt to create efficiencies and improve effectiveness.

Proposed Air Force Processes

Figure 3.2 shows the proposed process for new Air Force programs. Figure 3.3 shows the process for track 1 Air Force programs.

Figure 3.2
Proposed Process for New Air Force Programs

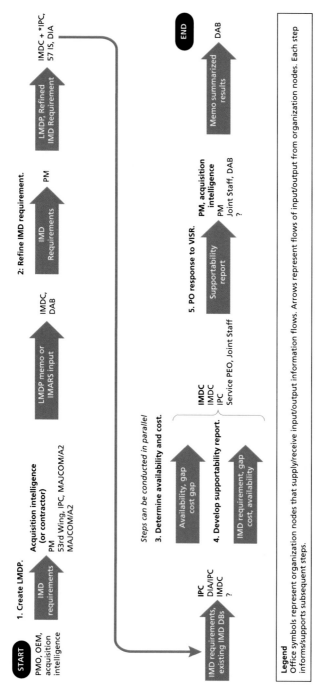

NOTES: DAB = Defense Acquisition Board; DIA = Defense Intelligence Agency; IS = Intelligence Squadron; MAJCOM/A2 = major command intelligence directorate; OEM = original equipment manufacturer; PM = program manager; PMO = Program Management Office; PO = program office; VISR = Validated IMD Supportability Report.

Figure 3.3
Proposed Process for Track 1 Air Force Programs

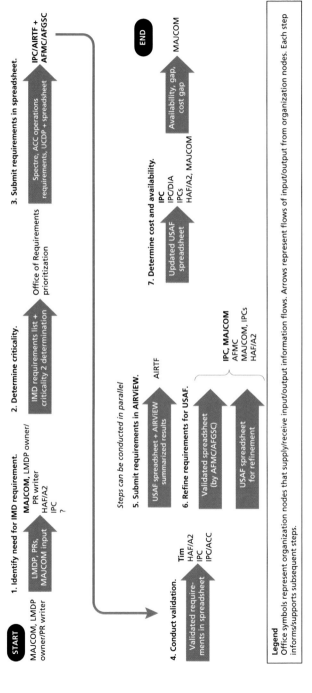

NOTES: ACC = Air Combat Command; AFGSC = Air Force Global Strike Command; AFMC = Air Force Materiel Command; DIA = Defense Intelligence Agency; HAF/A2 = Headquarters Air Force Intelligence Staff; MAJCOM = major command; UCDP = Uniform Collateral Data Portal; USAF = U.S. Air Force.

See Figure 3.4 for the proposed process for Air Force sustainment programs.

Proposed Army Processes

Figure 3.5 shows the proposed Army process for new programs.

Figure 3.6 shows the proposed process for Army sustainment programs.

Proposed Navy Processes

Figure 3.7 shows the proposed Navy process for new programs.

Figure 3.8 shows the proposed process for Navy sustainment programs.

Standardized Process Map

We propose that AIRTF consider the following 11 steps in a standardized process:

1. Characterize change in operational environment (major command or warfighter).
2. Determine Blue system vulnerability and Red system threat targets (acquisition and intelligence).
3. Identify IMD requirements (program manager, IMDC).
4. Enter IMD requirements into IMD tool (Program Management Office).
5. Refine IMD requirements (IMDC).
6. Validate IMD requirements (IPC).
7. Produce VISR (IMDC).
8. Determine availability and ability to fulfill requirements and cost (IPC).
9. Address gaps (IPC and Program Management Office).
10. Produce IPC's IMD (IPC).
11. Build mission data file (Program Management Office).

Figure 3.9 shows a standardized acquisition-intelligence process map.

Figure 3.4
Proposed Process for Air Force Sustainment Programs

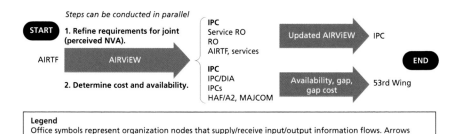

NOTES: DIA = Defense Intelligence Agency; HAF/A2 = Headquarter Air Force
Intelligence Staff; MAJCOM = major command; NVA = net value assessment;
RO = requirements officer.

Figure 3.5
Proposed Process for New Army Programs

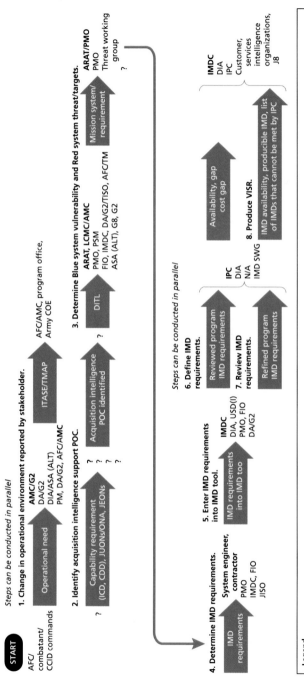

(Continued on next page)

Figure 3.5—Continued

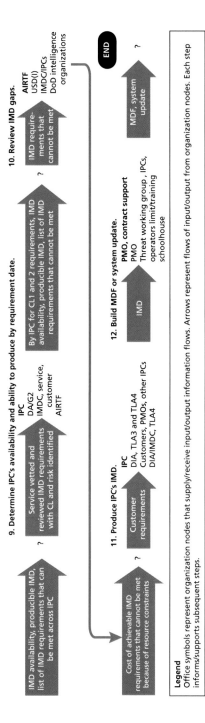

Legend

Office symbols represent organization nodes that supply/receive input/output information flows. Arrows represent flows of input/output information from organization nodes. Each step informs/supports subsequent steps.

NOTES: AFC = Army Futures Command; AMC/G2 = Army Materiel Command Directorate of Intelligence; ARAT = Army Reprogramming Analysis Team; ASA(ALT) = Assistant Secretary of the Army (Acquisitions, Technology, Logistics); CCID = Coalition Combat Identification; CDD = Capability Development Document; CL = criticality; COE = Corps of Engineers; DA/G2 = Department of the Army Directorate of Intelligence; DIA = Defense Intelligence Agency; DITL = Defense Intelligence Threat Library; FIO = foreign intelligence officer; G2 = U.S. Army Director of Intelligence; G8 = U.S. Army Director of Resource Management; ICD = Initial Capabilities Document; ITASE = Integrated Threat Analysis and Simulation Environment; J8 = Joint Chiefs of Staff Director of Force Structure, Resources, and Assessment; JEON = Joint Emergent Operational Need; JISO = Joint Intelligence Support Office; JUON = Joint Urgent Operational Need; LCMC = Life Cycle Mission Center; MDF = mission data file; N/A = not available; ONA = Office of Net Assessment; PM = program manager; PMO = Program Management Office; PSM = product support manager; SWG = Signals Working Group; TISO = Threat Intelligence Support Office; TLA = technology and long-range analysis; TLA3 = DIA Defense TLA Office for threat coordination; TLA4 = DIA Defense TLA Office for IMD coordination; TM = threat manager; TMAP = Threat Modeling and Analysis Program; USD(I) = Under Secretary of Defense for Intelligence; VISR = Validated IMD Supportability Report.

Figure 3.6
Proposed Process for Army Sustainment Programs

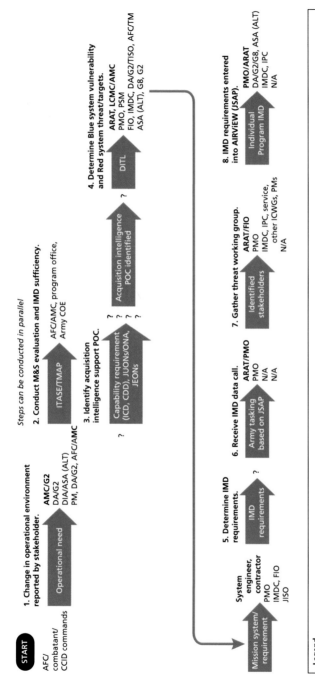

(Continued on next page)

Figure 3.6—Continued

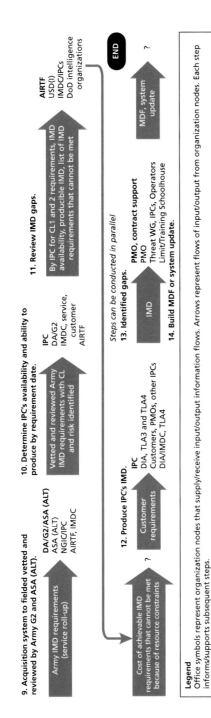

9. Acquisition system to fielded vetted and reviewed by Army G2 and ASA (ALT).

Army IMD requirements (service roll-up)

DA/G2/ASA (ALT)
ASA (ALT)
NGIC/IPC
AIRTF, IMDC

10. Determine IPC's availability and ability to produce by requirement date.

Vetted and reviewed Army IMD requirements with CL and risk identified

IPC
DA/G2
IMDC, service, customer
AIRTF

11. Review IMD gaps.

By IPC for CL1 and 2 requirements, IMD availability, producible IMD, list of IMD requirements that cannot be met

AIRTF
USD(I)
IMDC/IPCs
DoD intelligence organizations

END

Cost of achievable IMD requirements that cannot be met because of resource constraints

?

12. Produce IPC's IMD.

Customer requirements

IPC
DIA, TLA3 and TLA4
Customers, PMOs, other IPCs
DIA/IMDC, TLA4

Steps can be conducted in parallel

13. Identified gaps.

IMD

PMO, contract support
PMO
Threat WG, IPCs, Operators
Limit/Training Schoolhouse

14. Build MDF or system update.

MDF, system update

?

Legend
Office symbols represent organization nodes that supply/receive input/output information flows. Arrows represent flows of input/output from organization nodes. Each step informs/supports subsequent steps.

NOTES: AFC = Army Futures Command; AMC/G2 = Army Materiel Command Directorate of Intelligence; ARAT = Army Reprogramming Analysis Team; ASA(ALT) = Assistant Secretary of the Army (Acquisitions, Technology, Logistics); CCID = Coalition Combat Identification; CDD = Capability Development Document; CL = criticality; COE = Corps of Engineers; DA/G2 = Department of the Army Directorate of Intelligence; DIA = Defense Intelligence Agency; DITL = Defense Intelligence Threat Library; FIO = foreign intelligence officer; G8 = U.S. Army Director of Resource Management; ICD = Initial Capabilities Document; ICWG = Interface Control Working Group; ITASE = Integrated Threat Analysis and Simulation Environment; JEON = Joint Emergent Operational Need; JISO = Joint Intelligence Support Office; JSAP = Joint Staff Action Package; JUON = Joint Urgent Operational Need; LCMC = Life Cycle Mission Center; MDF = mission data file; M&S = Modeling and Simulation; NGIC = National Ground Intelligence Center; ONA = Office of Net Assessment; PM = Program Manager; PMO = Program Management Office; PSM = product support manager; TISO = Threat Intelligence Support Office; TLA = technology and long-range analysis; TLA3 = DIA Defense TLA Office for threat coordination; TLA4 = DIA Defense TLA Office for IMD coordination; TM = threat manager; TMAP = Threat Modeling and Analysis Program; USD(I) = Under Secretary of Defense for Intelligence; WG = working group.

Figure 3.7
Proposed Process for New Navy Programs

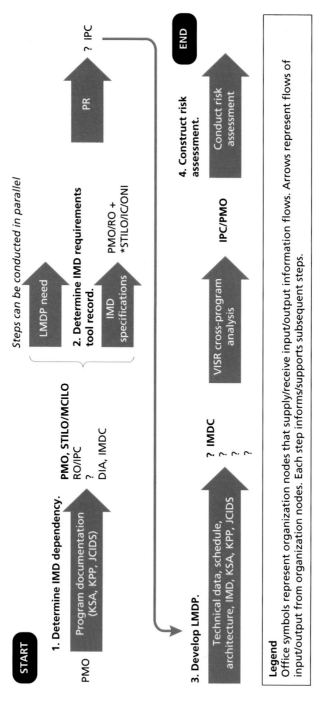

Legend
Office symbols represent organization nodes that supply/receive input/output information flows. Arrows represent flows of input/output from organization nodes. Each step informs/supports subsequent steps.

NOTES: DAB = Defense Acquisition Board; DIA = Defense Intelligence Agency; IS = Intelligence Squadron; KPP = key performance parameter; KSA = key system attribute; MAJCOM/A2 = major command intelligence directorate; MCILO = Marine Corps intelligence liaison officer; OEM = original equipment manufacturer; ONI = Office of Naval Intelligence; PM = program manager; PMO = Program Management Office; PO = program office; RO = requirements officer; STILO = science and technology intelligence liaison officer; VISR = Validated IMD Supportability Report.

Figure 3.8
Proposed Process for Navy Sustainment Programs

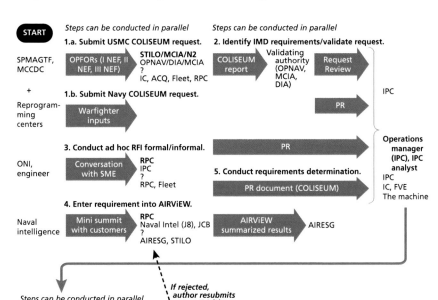

Legend
Office symbols represent organization nodes that supply/receive input/output information flows. Arrows represent flows of input/output from organization nodes. Each step informs/supports subsequent steps.

NOTES: ACQ = acquisition; AIRESG = Acquisition Intelligence Requirements Executive Steering Group; DIA = Defense Intelligence Agency; FVE = Five Eyes alliance; IDIP = Integrated Defense Intelligence Priorities; J8 = Joint Staff, Director of Force Structure, Resources, and Assessment; JCB = Joint Capabilities Board; MCCDC = Marine Corps Combat Development Command; MCIA = Marine Corps Intelligence Activity; N2 = U.S. Navy Directorate of Intelligence; NEF = Naval Expeditionary Force; NIPF = National Intelligence Priorities Framework; ONI = Office of Naval Intelligence; OPFOR = operating force; OPNAV = Office of the Chief of Naval Operations; POA = program of analysis; RFI = request for information; RPC = Regional Processing Center; SPMAGTF = Special Purpose Marine Air-Ground Task Force; STILO = science and technology intelligence liaison officer; USMC = U.S. Marine Corps.

Figure 3.9
Proposed IMD Development Process for New Programs and Programs in Sustainment

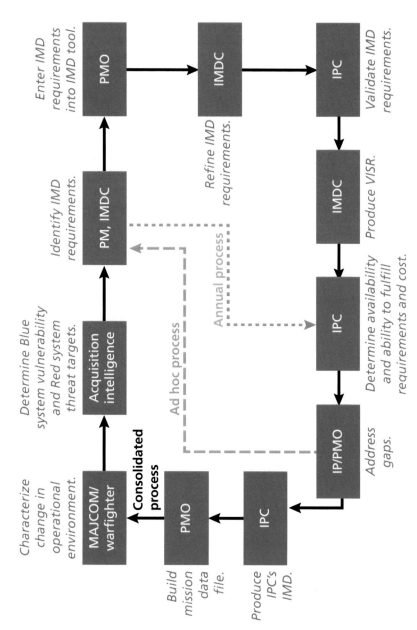

CHAPTER FOUR

Observations, Suggestions, and Further Research

Observations

1. A standardized and effective acquisition-intelligence governance process is lacking, as is an accepted practice for developing IMD requirements and translating them into intelligence tasks.

The DoDI 5250.02 requirement for developing the LMDP document provides specific guidance to stakeholders to identify IMD requirements and to ascertain whether intelligence can support the tasks. The process for moving these tasks forward, however, is less clear. The plethora of departmental and service documents do not, in their totality, provide processes or standards that can be used, especially by intelligence support officers who identify IMD requirements and ensure that they are communicated to the appropriate intelligence organization for action. The instructions and regulations that exist do not provide specific or sufficient guidance about how IMD requirements are to be processed once they are identified.

2. There appear to be too many stakeholders involved in the IMD task-development process, and their responsibilities are ill defined.

It is unclear what the responsibilities are for stakeholders during the process with advisory, coordinating, or information access. The absence of any identifiable governance document suggests that these responsibilities may be defined differently by different programs and military departments and that the definition of responsibilities may change over time as individual players rotate through the system.

3. The IMD requirements-identification and production-development process comprises two distinct phases that vary by service.

Data from the CPI event and our work to develop process wire frames depict this complicated process. They identify large numbers of stakeholders in the process who have varying inputs to the system. We used the data collected at the CPI event as a basis for analysis using the RACI approach to assign roles and responsibilities for each aspect of the wire frame diagram to map out roles for each entity involved and reduce confusion. RAND analysis concluded that this process occurs in two phases. The first phase is largely driven by the acquisition community (the LMDP) or operators, while the second phase is almost entirely an intelligence process (PR developing and tasking). Intelligence support personnel play critical but collaborative roles in both processes; they are not the actual users of the intelligence provided to customers, but neither are they the producers of that intelligence. The requirement to function in two different communities may lead to the kinds of process impediments revealed in the CPI event and in the wire frames. It places specific requirements on these personnel who are expected to understand both communities and to translate tasks and concepts between them. The AIRTF already understands the need for more-specialized training for intelligence support personnel in these roles. This analysis suggests that additional training, coupled with additional and specific governance documents at all levels, could reduce process impediments.

4. IMD requirements can generally be binned into three categories: long-term requirements generally associated with an acquisition program; ad hoc requirements that come from CCMDs and operational forces; and requirements that are identified in the annual plan review of IMD requirements.

Each category has different processes for requirement validation and tasking. Moreover, it appears that each service has different approaches to the three categories of requirements, a situation that further complicates the picture. Each of these processes, however, eventually ends up in a validated production requirement that should likely appear in COLISEUM. The tasks are unique to service IPCs and may not be registered there. The absence of a single "demand signal repository" for IMD requirements has several implications. At the operational level, validators are unable to avoid duplicate tasks because they may not have knowledge tasks or access to databases holding them. At a management level, planners and senior managers seeking to resource and manage more-strategic IC processes lack comprehensive data on which to make future programming decisions. In both cases, the IC falls short of having the ability to avoid unnecessary work or to plan resources and expertise for future requirements that may be levied by operational and other military consumers.

5. Guidance on PR introduction and processing is obsolete.

The *Department of Defense Intelligence Production Program: Requirements Management* document from November 1998 provides the most comprehensive guidance on how PRs are introduced into and processed through the system, but it has not been updated to keep pace with changes that have occurred. The guidance was prepared for a different intelligence production program that no longer exists; it is likely obsolete and is no longer used widely as guidance. Many of the concepts and processes, however, remain relevant. For example, it contains useful definitions that likely remain current, such as its guidance on PR validation responsibilities and how PRs are most effectively written. Poorly written requirements are often the source of delays in production. This finding was echoed in—and the process impediments identified at—the CPI meeting. Our research did not discover any guidance on standard action timelines other than those included in the 1998 document. The timelines strike us as reasonable for most, although not all, production tasks. Ad hoc tasks for data needed immediately to support operations or planning are tighter than routine long-term production timelines and thus should receive higher-priority production attention.

6. Some COLISEUM fields could be automated to improve standardization of inputs and ensure better-quality tasking inputs, add precision to tasks, and facilitate movement of tasks between systems, thus improving the timeliness and quality of IMD products.

Information on COLISEUM acquired during previous research indicates that COLISEUM can link to other databases to share common information. Some demographic data are likely easy to be shared if appropriate application program interfaces are developed and approved for use on classified systems. It would be more difficult to automate the IFCs that direct the task to the appropriate producer. Other codes embedded in COLISEUM, which are used to gather production data for management and other purposes, might also be difficult to automate. Additionally, using automated data transfer to move a requirement from one system to another might result in a task that cannot be acted on by intelligence producers.

Suggestions

We developed several suggestions based on the observations provided.

1. Focus less on the acquisition side of the acquisition-intelligence process and more on the intelligence side, where impact is more likely.

Once the military departments have completed work on the LMDP, the requirement moves into the intelligence environment, where IMD requirements can be misinterpreted and/or misdirected. Fulfilling the production requirements often calls for the active collaboration of several intelligence organizations; the DIAP identifies the production "lanes in the road," the guide used to divide intelligence requirements into actual production tasks. There are many points of inefficiency in this process now. There is no strong governance that establishes standards for activity. The validation process is critical to ensuring effectiveness, and validators are tasked to provide critical expertise to the process. As just noted, individuals managing the tasks in COLISEUM do not always have the substantive expertise to discharge their responsibilities successfully. Establishing detailed guidance for this professional specialty would go a long way in resolving some of the friction that currently exists in the system. Similarly, existing AIRTF work on developing new training and professional development opportunities for career intelligence liaison and acquisition intelligence officers would further improve the process.

2. Create a "demand signal repository" by exploring direct electronic connections among the tools and databases currently used to manage IMD issues.

There are various tools and databases currently used to manage identification and fulfillment of IMD needs, including IMARS, AIRViEW, COLISEUM, and service-specific systems. These databases and tools were developed to achieve specific purposes and to provide outputs, but none of them currently has the data, the task, or likely the capability to serve as a central IMD requirements database that can be used to manage tasks and to provide oversight officials with the comprehensive data they need to develop data-driven resource, expertise, and policy decisions. Before considering the development or acquisition of a new tool, efforts should be made to determine whether connections among existing tools would provide the needed capability.

3. Use the upcoming CPI event to seek consensus on the priorities laid out in this report.

The most-recent CPI event identified many issues—so many, in fact, that it would be extremely difficult to prioritize them. The upcoming CPI event might focus only on the issues unique to IC involvement in the process, which is what we suggest would likely produce the most gains.

4. Consider drafting an IMD manual, similar to the JCIDS manual, to capture processes and standard operating procedures for IMD professionals.

The AIRTF previously undertook a rewrite of DoDI 5250. Our analysis of governance documents, however, revealed that although some provide guidance on IMD activities, none clarifies the major concepts underpinning IMD activities or provides sufficiently detailed and standardized process characterizations to be used by all stakeholders.

5. Adopt the RAND-developed process maps.

Analysis of the CPI data led RAND to develop streamlined process maps that could be used as a basis for making existing processes more efficient and effective by eliminating some unnecessary steps. We developed these alternative processes with the concept of making processes sequential and ensuring that each process set up the succeeding process for success.

Further Research

In addition to the issues noted in the observations and suggestions provided in this chapter, there are additional areas where further research is warranted and would likely yield positive results:

- Although we presented some material on LMDP and ad hoc requirements, we were unable to review in detail the annual plan requirements. This should be done to round out the three processes and would allow us to respond more fully to the question, "What are the equities of the stakeholders (i.e., customers and producers)?"
- Without interviewing system users, we were not able to answer the question, "Is there preference for automated COLISEUM input?" We think this would likely provide significant value.
- It is not clear that the validation process puts enough emphasis on the original tasking organization for researching existing intelligence or to ensure that the requirement has not been duplicated. Thus, we were unable to answer the question, "Service processes for validating the requirement: When is a PR necessary?"
- The aspect of splitting tasks is likely an area where inefficiencies may occur and where time is spent managing the process rather than focusing on analysis. Although we assess there is sufficient data to gain insight into splitting tasks, we were unable to research this issue. Analysis of a select number of these records could identify systemic problems that could possibly be ameliorated or eliminated with new or revised policies.
- We could not confirm whether the required timelines for post-PR validation processes are being observed. We think this has value and could be accomplished through analysis of IMD-related tasks in COLISEUM.

- Investigating the question "Are there business plan changes that could resolve an ad hoc PR before making it part of the annual plan (e.g. what are urgent needs and how should they be conveyed)?" could yield the greatest benefit, as there is no demand signal repository-like capability in the IC for managing the intelligence-tasking part of the equation. Given the large numbers of these tasks, additional review of processes with the IMDC and the reprogramming labs would likely be enlightening. Although limited time and resources prevented us from reviewing this question in any detail, analysis of the current processes using actual tasking data might reveal insights that could reduce impediments and improve overall effectiveness.

- The LMDP process appears to be different in each service. It is somewhat well described in the Air Force but appears to be less so in the Army and Navy. Generally, the process is not captured in governance documents. We determined, for instance, that IMD requirements for Navy programs funnel through a single office that ensures tasks are actionable, not duplicative, and reasonable. The Army, however, does not appear to have a similar process and limited time and funding prevented us from further researching this. Additional effort would allow us more fully to answer the question, "Can the amount of input be reduced and by what order or magnitude?"

References

Chairman of the Joint Chiefs of Staff, *Charter of the Joint Requirements Oversight Council (JROC) and Implementation of the Joint Capabilities Integration and Development System (JCIDS)*, Washington, D.C., August 31, 2018.

Chairman of the Joint Chiefs of Staff Instruction 3000, draft of IMD prioritization, undated, Not available to the general public.

Chairman of the Joint Chiefs of Staff Instruction 3170.01I, *Joint Capabilities Integration and Development System (JCIDS)*, Washington, D.C., January 23, 2015.

Chairman of the Joint Chiefs of Staff Instruction 3901.01D, *Requirements for Geospatial Information and Services*, Washington, D.C., March 29, 2013, Not available to the general public.

Chairman of the Joint Chiefs of Staff Instruction 3210.03, *Joint Electronic Warfare Policy*. Washington, D.C., undated, Not available to the general public.

Chairman of the Joint Chiefs of Staff Instruction 3320.01D, *Joint Electromagnetic Spectrum Operations (JEMSO)*, Washington, D.C., January 21, 2013.

Chairman of the Joint Chiefs of Staff Instruction 5123.01H, *Charter of the Joint Requirements Oversight Council (JROC) and Implementation of the Joint Capabilities Integration and Development System (JCIDS)*, Washington, D.C., August 31, 2018.

Chairman of the Joint Chiefs of Staff Instruction 6212.01F, *Net Ready Key Performance Parameter (NR KPP)*, Washington, D.C., March 21, 2012. As of July 22, 2020:
http://www.acqnotes.com/Attachments/CJCSI%206212.01F%20Net%20Ready%20Key%20Performance%20Parameter%20(NR%20KPP)%2012%20March%2012.pdf

Chief of Naval Operations Instruction 3811.1F, *Threat Support to the Defense Acquisition System*, Washington, D.C.: Department of the Navy, Office of the Chief of Naval Operations, May 16, 2016. As of July 22, 2020:
https://www.secnav.navy.mil/doni/Directives/03000%20Naval%20Operations%20and%20Readiness/03-800%20Intelligence%20Support/3811.1F.pdf

Chief of Naval Operations Instruction 3880.6A, *Scientific and Technical Intelligence Liaison Officer (STILO) Program and Intelligence Support for the Naval Research, Development, Test and Evaluation, and Acquisition Communities*, Washington, D.C.: Department of the Navy, Office of the Chief of Naval Operations, November 5, 2007. As of July 22, 2020: https://www.secnav.navy.mil/doni/Directives/03000%20Naval%20Operations%20and%20Readiness/03-800%20Intelligence%20Support/3880.6A.pdf

Defense Acquisition University, *Defense Acquisition Guidebook*, Fort Belvoir, Va., February 26, 2017. As of July 22, 2020: https://www.dau.edu/tools/t/Defense-Acquisition-Guidebook

Defense Acquisition University, "Program Management: DAU Sponsored Documents," webpage ("Benefits of DoDD 5250.01 & IMD Planning Process for the Acquisition Community [AC]"), June 1, 2017. As of September 6, 2020: https://www.dau.edu/cop/pm/DAU%20Sponsored%20Documents/Forms/Reference.aspx?Paged=TRUE&p_SortBehavior=0&p_Modified=20170602%2002%3A13%3A10&p_ID=470&PageFirstRow=301&&View=%7B2A9F19F8-A7D6-4780-8C1F-A85121F1F8D1%7D

Defense Intelligence Agency, Defense Technology and Long-Range Analysis Office, *Intelligence Mission Data Cost Methodology Guidebook*, Fort Belvoir, Va., January 22, 2013.

Defense Intelligence Agency, Defense Technology and Long-Range Analysis Office, *Life-Cycle Mission Data Plan (LMDP) Guidebook and Templates*, Version 3.1, Fort Belvoir, Va., April 8, 2014. As of September 6, 2020: https://www.dau.edu/cop/pm/DAU%20Sponsored%20Documents/LMDP%20Guidebook%20v3.1.pdf

Defense Intelligence Agency Instruction 5000.002, *Defense Intelligence Threat Support for Major Defense Acquisition Programs*, rescinded, Washington, D.C., June 19, 2019, Not available to the general public.

Defense Intelligence Management Document DoD-0000-151C-98, *Department of Defense Intelligence Production Program: Requirements Management*, 1998, No longer available to the general public.

Department of the Air Force, Air Force Instruction 10-703, *Electronic Warfare (EW) Integrated Reprogramming*, Washington, D.C., June 4, 2014, Incorporating Change 1, February 22, 2017.

Department of the Air Force, Air Force Instruction 14-111, *Intelligence Support to the Acquisition Life-Cycle*, Washington, D.C., May 18, 2012, Incorporating Change 1, June 16, 2014 (rescinded).

Department of the Army, Army Regulation 381-11, *Intelligence Support to Capability Development*, Washington, D.C., January 30, 2019.

Department of Defense Directive 3222.04, *Electronic Warfare (EW) Policy*, Washington, D.C., March 26, 2014, Incorporating Change 2, August 31, 2018.

Department of Defense Directive 5250.01, *Management of Intelligence Mission Data (IMD) in DoD Acquisition*, Washington, D.C., January 22, 2013, Incorporating Change 1, August 29, 2017. As of July 20, 2020:
https://www.esd.whs.mil/Portals/54/Documents/DD/issuances/dodd/525001p.pdf

Department of Defense Instruction 5000.02T, *Operation of the Defense Acquisition System*, Washington, D.C., January 7, 2015, Incorporating Change 7, April 21, 2020. As of July 22, 2020:
https://www.esd.whs.mil/Portals/54/Documents/DD/issuances/dodi/500002T
.pdf?ver=2020-04-22-083324-963

Department of Defense Instruction 5000.56, *Programming Geospatial-Intelligence (GEOINT), Geospatial Information and Services (GI&S), and Geodesy Requirements for Developing Systems*, Washington, D.C., July 9, 2010, Incorporating Change 1, September 25, 2017. As of July 22, 2020:
https://fas.org/irp/doddir/dod/i5000_56.pdf

DoD—*See* U.S. Department of Defense.

DoDD—*See* Department of Defense Directive.

DoDI—*See* Department of Defense Instruction.

Gartner, "Gartner Glossary: Demand Signal Repository (DSR)," website, undated. As of July 22, 2020:
https://www.gartner.com/en/information-technology/glossary
/demand-signal-repository-dsr

Harned, Brett, "How to Clear Project Confusion with a RACI Chart [Template]," Team Gantt webpage, September 16, 2019. As of September 6, 2020:
https://www.teamgantt.com/blog/raci-chart-definition-tips-and-example

Joint Capabilities Integration and Development System Manual, *Manual for the Operation of the Joint Capabilities Integration and Development System (JCIDS)*, Appendix I, Enclosure D, p. D-I-10. As of September 30, 2020:
http://www.acqnotes.com/wp-content/uploads/2014/09/Manual-for-the
-Operationsof-the-Joint-Capabilities-Integration-and
-Development-System-JCIDS-18-Dec-2015.pdf

Marine Corps Systems Command, MARCORSYSCOM Acquisition Guidebook 5000.3B, *Implementation of Marine Corps Systems Command Acquisition Tools*, August 14, 2015, updated February 3, 2017, Not available to the general public.

National Air and Space Intelligence Center Instruction 10-102, *Issue Manager Instructions*, Wright-Patterson Air Force Base, Ohio, undated.

OPNAVINST—*See* Chief of Naval Operations Instruction.

Under Secretary of Defense for Acquisition, Technology, and Logistics, *Implementation Directive for Better Buying Power 3.0: Achieving Dominant Capabilities Through Technical Excellence and Innovation*, Washington, D.C., April 9, 2015. As of July 10, 2020:
https://www.acq.osd.mil/fo/docs/betterBuyingPower3.0(9Apr15).pdf

U.S. Department of Defense, *Department of Defense Intelligence Production Program: Requirements Management*, Washington, D.C., November 1998, Not available to the general public.

U.S. Department of Defense, *DOD Dictionary of Military and Associated Terms*, Washington, D.C., June 2020.

U.S. Government Accountability Office, *Defense Intelligence: Additional Steps Could Better Integrate Intelligence Input into DOD's Acquisition of Major Weapon Systems*, Washington, D.C., GAO-17-10, November 2016. As of July 10, 2020:
https://www.gao.gov/assets/690/680735.pdf